BIRMINGHAM
TO
TAMWORTH
and NUNEATON

Vic Mitchell

MP Middleton Press

Front cover: Tips were typical in many types of industrial areas with which this album deals. Class 4F 0-6-0 no. 44260 is hard at work at Bromford Bridge on 2nd March 1963. (Colour-Rail.com)

Back cover upper: Nuneaton Abbey Street is the location of this record of steam at its optimum. Class 8F 2-8-0s nos. 48584 and 48111 run west. No date was recorded. (Colour-Rail.com)

Back cover centre: This 1910 diagram unravels the complexity of routes in the Birmingham area. Our route is top right. (Railway Clearing House)

Back cover lower: Nos 20157 and 20166 pass through Water Orton's up platform on 5th June 1980. No. 47015 waits at the end of the up goods line. (A.C.Hartless)

Published July 2014

ISBN 978 1 908174 63 5

© *Middleton Press, 2014*

Design Deborah Esher
Typesetting Barbara Mitchell

Published by
Middleton Press
Easebourne Lane
Midhurst
West Sussex
GU29 9AZ
Tel: 01730 813169
Fax: 01730 812601
Email: info@middletonpress.co.uk
www.middletonpress.co.uk

Printed in the United Kingdom by Henry Ling Limited, at the Dorset Press, Dorchester, DT1 1HD

INDEX

I. The Railway Clearing House map is from 1947.
Please see the back cover for earlier ownership details of the western area.

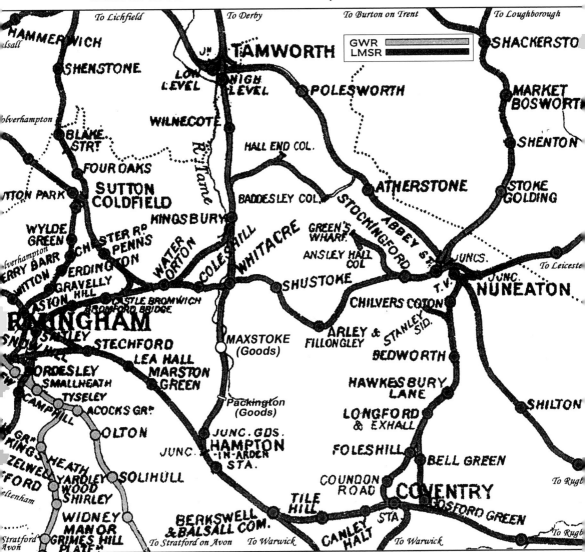

ACKNOWLEDGEMENTS

I am very grateful for the assistance received from many of those mentioned in the credits, also to A.R.Carder, G.Croughton, S.Davies, S.C.Jenkins, Mr D. and Dr S.Salter, T.Walsh and in particular Barbara Mitchell, my ever caring wife.

GEOGRAPHICAL SETTING

The iron and coal of the Midlands allowed Birmingham to develop its manufacturing industries and grow to become Britain's second largest city. The River Tame runs eastwards north of the city centre, before turning north after passing Water Orton. Running roughly parallel to it is the Birmingham & Fazeley Canal, which helped the district to flourish in the pre-railway era.

The route between Water Orton and Nuneaton is more steeply graded and passes over a ridge containing coal measures, which have been very productive. The coalfield is approximately two miles wide by ten miles north-south. Elsewhere, the lines were laid mostly over sandstones, but all were within Warwickshire.

The route south of Water Orton to Hampton-in-Arden was close to the north flowing tributary of the Tame, the River Blythe.

The scale of the maps is 25ins to 1 mile and north is at the top unless otherwise indicated.

MR Gradient Profiles.

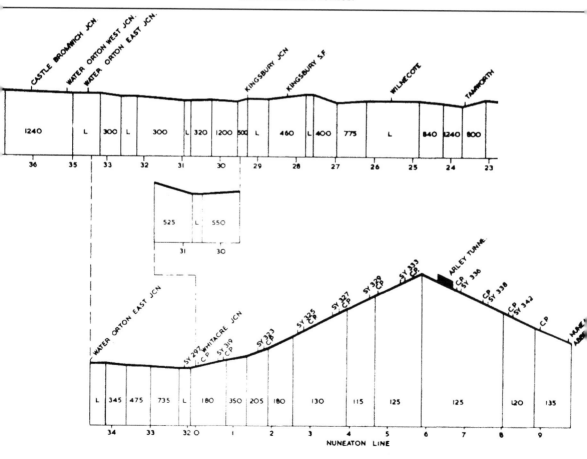

HISTORICAL BACKGROUND

The Birmingham & Derby Junction Railway gained its Act in 1836 and opened on 12th August 1839. A branch south from Whitacre to Hampton opened at the same time and provided a link with the London & Birmingham Railway. A service was operated between Derby and Euston until 1845, when a more direct route became available. The slow demise of the link is detailed later.

The L&BR was built under an Act of 1833 and trains ran into Birmingham Curzon Street from 24th June 1838. The Grand Junction Railway ran from here from 1837 to provide a link with the 1830 Liverpool & Manchester Railway at Warrington. Curzon Street was replaced by Birmingham New Street in 1854. This had been brought into use for Wolverhampton trains via Tipton on 1st July 1852. All were operated by the London & North Western Railway, which had taken over the L&BR and the GJR upon its formation in 1846.

The B&DJR became part of the Midland Railway in 1844. The LNWR linked Rugby and Stafford with a line running through Nuneaton and Tamworth in 1847.

The MR extended from Water Orton to Nuneaton on 1st November 1864. Here it met the 1862 South Leicestershire Railway from Hinckley and trains ran on to Leicester from 1864. The Ashby & Nuneaton Joint Committee arranged services between these places from 1873. Nuneaton was provided with trains from Coventry by the LNWR from 1850.

The MR and the LNWR became the main constituents of the London Midland & Scottish Railway in 1923. Most of this became the London Midland Region of British Railways upon nationalisation in 1948.

Privatisation resulted in some services between Birmingham and Derby being franchised to Cross Country, part of the Virgin Group, from January 1997. Arriva retained the name Cross Country, when it took over in November 2007. The same route and also the line to Nuneaton was used by Central Trains from March 1997. From November 2007, this was also Cross Country operated.

The goods yard operations are detailed in the captions.

PASSENGER SERVICES

The train frequencies on the routes are shown in sample years, but only those running on more than five days per week. The wide range of destinations is indicated in the captions.

Birmingham to Tamworth				
	Fast		Most Stations	
	Weekdays	Sundays	Weekdays	Sundays
1845	3	1	3	2
1869	6	2	4	2
1899	9	3	3	2
1929	10	3	5	2
1959	18	7	5	4
1998	21	9	13	0

Birmingham to Nuneaton				
	Fast		Most Stations	
	Weekdays	Sundays	Weekdays	Sundays
1869	3	1	4	2
1899	12	5	3	2
1929	5	0	7	2
1959	3	0	13	9
1998	28	9	0	0

Whitacre to Hampton

When part of the main line in the first three years of its life, the route carried three trains (Sundays two initially, but more later) and these contained through coaches to Euston until February 1845. Thereafter, there were three local trains, these being reduced to two in 1859. There were six in 1869, but only one from 1871. This lasted until 1917, when passenger service ceased on the route.

BIRMINGHAM & DERBY JUNCTION.

Miles	DERBY TO BIRMINGHAM AND LONDON. STATIONS.	*Mixed, 8 25 a.m.*	*mixed 11 45 a.m.*	*mixed 2 15 p.m.*	*mixed 4 30 p.m.*	*1st & 2d class mail, 11 p.m.*	Sunday Trains. *Mixed, 8 a.m.*	*mixed 5½ p.m.*	*1st & 2nd Class, mail, 11 p.m.*
	DERBY	8 25	11 45	2 15	4 30	11 0	8 0	5 30	11 0
6¼	Willington ..	8 37	..	2 27	4 42	..	8 12	5 42	..
11	BURTON	8 49	12 5	2 38	4 52	11 25	8 23	5 53	11 25
14¾	Barton & Walton	9 0	12 23	2 56	5 2	..	8 41	6 11	..
17¾	Oakley & Alrewas	9 8	12 30	3 2	5 12	..	8 47	6 17	..
24	TAMWORTH ..	9 20	12 48	3 20	5 27	11 55	9 5	6 35	11 55
29½	Kingsbury ..	9 35	..	3 35	5 41	..	9 20	6 50	..
33¼	Coleshill	9 47	1 13	3 46	5 53	..	9 31	7 1	..
38½	HAMPTON, Arrival at	10 5	1 30	4 10	6 15	12 25	9 55	7 25	12 25
47¾	BIRMINGHAM	10 40	2 0	4 30	6 45	1 0	10 15	7 45	1 0
	LONDON	3 15	6 30	9 15	11 30	..	..	..	..

The 8 25 a.m. train is in connexion with one from Nottingham at 7 30 a.m.; the 11 45 a.m. with one from York at 6 45 a.m.; the 2 15 p.m. train with one from Darlington at 5 45 a.m.; the 4 30 p.m. with one at 9 45 a.m.; and the 11 p m. with the one at 3 p.m.

January 1841

January 1845

Mls.	UP TRAINS. STATIONS	Derby to Birmingham and London. 1	2	3	4	5	6	7 &10	Sundays. 8
								mail	
	Departure from	a.m.	a.m.	p.m.	p.m	p.m.	p.m	p m	a. m.
	DERBY	8 15	10 30	12 15	2 0	4 40	8 15	10 50	8 30
6½	Willington	8 25	..	12 25	..	4 50	8 25	..	8 40
11	**Burton**	8 35	10 50	12 35	2 20	5 0	8 35	11 13	8 50
15	Barton & Walton	8 45	11 0	12 45	..	5 10	8 45	..	9 0
17¾	Oakley & Alrewas	8 55	11 10	12 50	2 30	5 18	8 55	..	9 10
24	**Tamworth** ..	9 10	11 30	1 10	3 0	5 35	9 15	11 50	9 28
25¾	Wilncote&Fazly.	9 15	..	1 15	..	5 40	9 20	..	9 34
29¾	Kingsbury......	9 30	..	1 25	.	5 50	9 30	..	9 43
31¼	Whitacre Junc..	9 35	11 45	1 30	3 20	5 55	9 35	..	9 48
33	Forge Mills	9 40	11 50	1 35	..	6 2	9 40	..	9 55
34½	Water Orton....	9 45	..	1 40	..	6 10	..	..	10 0
37	Castle Bromwich	9 50	..	1 45	..	6 15	9 50	..	..
41¼	**Birmingham**	10 20	12 30	2 15	4 0	6 30	10 15	12 35	10 20
33¼	Coleshill........	9 40	11 50	..	3 25	..	..	..	..
38½	**Hampton**....	10 10	12 10	..	3 45	..	..	..	..
47½	**Coventry**....	10 44	12 49	..	4 59	..	..	..	..
141½	**LONDON**....	2 45	5 15	..	8 45	..	..	..	..

FARES, FROM BIRMINGHAM

TO	1 Cls. s. d.	2 Cls. s. d.	3 Cls. s. d.	TO	1 Cls. s. d.	2 Cls. s. d.	3 Cls. s. d.
Nottingham ..	14 6	10 6	—	Tamworth....	4 0	3 0	2 0
Leeds	31 0	22 0	—	Barton&Waltn	7 6	5 6	4 6
York	35 6	25 6	—	Burton	7 6	5 6	4 6
Hull	38 6	28 6	—	Derby........	11 0	8 0	6 0
Darlington....	48 6	34 6	—	Sheffield......	23 0	16 0	—

BIRMINGHAM NEW STREET

II.   The 1946 edition at 6ins to 1 mile has New Street station lower left and the GWR's Moor Street station to the right of it. Curzon Street Goods Depot is to the right of centre. This had been the terminus of the L&BR from 1838 until 1st July 1854, when trains ran into New Street from the east for the first time. Our route is the lower one on the right. It continues on the map near picture 10.

1.   No details are available, but it seems appropriate to start with an atmospheric shot from the late Victorian period, particularly as it contains a six-wheeled coach of the era. (P.Laming coll.)

2.   Originally platforms 1 to 6 were LNWR property and the others belonged to the MR. However, the footbridge was a public right of way across the entire station. (P.Laming coll.)

3.   Both this picture and the previous one show a platform numbering which does not match the one shown on the next diagram. This is probably a London-bound express at the later No. 3. The leading locomotive is "Waterloo" class no. 36 *Thalaba*. (P.Laming coll.)

III.   Upper is the layout prior to the rebuilding in the mid-1960s. Lower is the arrangement after complete electrification in 1966. Our route is the right one at the top. The southern tunnel at the east of the station was completed in 1896 and is 254 yards in length.

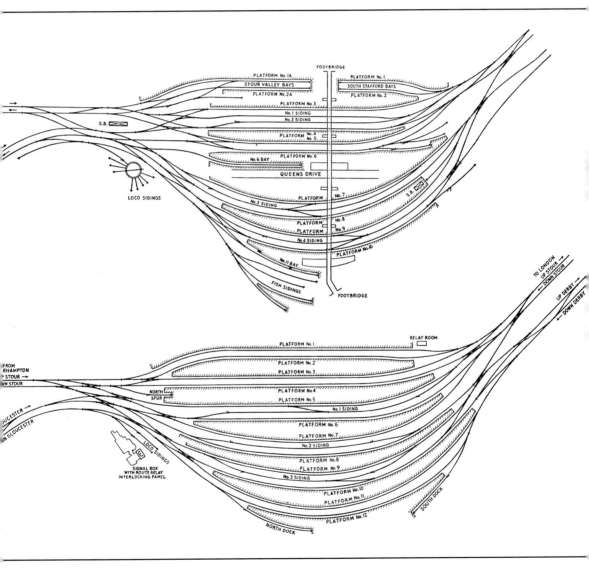

4.   The overall glazed roof suffered severely in the bombing of World War II and some canopiesof this type were built from 1948 onwards, but funds were very limited. This northward view from 2nd June 1962 has the Queens Hotel in the background and the SLS "Sutton Coldfield Centenary" tour centre stage. It was hauled by class 8F 0-8-0 no. 48930 and ran via Sutton Coldfield, Aston, Stechford, New Street, Wednesbury Town, Dudley Port and was back to New Street in 3 hours 37 minutes. (B.S.Jennings)

5.   This panorama from 3rd May 1965 of the rebuilding is southeastwards and includes details of the short-lived roofing. Also evident is No. 2 signal box, which lasted until 1966. (Colour-Rail.com)

6.   This is the east end of the station on 8th January 1983, as EMU no. 312203 waits to leave for Walsall at 11.12. The new design created an extensive retail area, but a low ceiling over the platforms gave a depressing ambience, especially on sunny days. DMUs began running to Nuneaton and Leicester in March 1958. (A.C.Hartless)

7. The new Stephenson Street entrance, located in the northwest corner of the redevelopment, is shown in February 2014, prior to the full completion of the reflective cladding panels. This entrance was opened at the "half-way" stage of the re-development on 28th April 2013. (I.Pell)

8.   We now have a view of the eastern elevation of the station, with building work in progress on 4th February 2014. The frame is where the old 1965 station forecourt was. This area will be fully clad, similar to the Stephenson Street entrance. On the extreme right, just visible at low level, are the running lines. By 2014, the station carried 140,000 passengers per day, over double the capacity for which the 1960s development was designed. (I.Pell)

BIRMINGHAM CURZON STREET

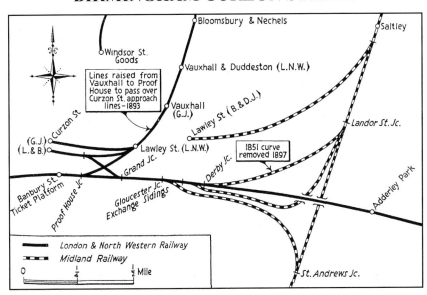

IV.   A pre-1923 diagram helps to locate the junctions and indicates the positions of the original termini on the left. The third terminus is near the centre; Lawley Street served passengers from 1842 to 1851. An inclined plane linked the L&BR and GJR for freight traffic in 1842-43. Derby Junction is now known as Grand Junction and is where overhead electrification ends on our journey. (Railway Magazine)

9.   This is the east end of Curzon Street Goods Depot in around 1950 and two white columns indicate the position of the original passenger station, which still stands. Its frontage appears in picture 76 in *North of Birmingham*. (Warwickshire Railways Society coll.)

V.　　This continuation of map II has the eastern half of Lawley Street Goods Depot lower left and our route running to the right of the upper border. Saltley is marked unclearly, above centre and near the overbridge marked Saltley Viaduct. The River Rea runs close to the route. The extensive works to the right is that of the Metropolitan - Cammell Carriage & Wagon Company. It also has a connection to the Aston to Stechford line, which is diagonally top right and is now electrified. Below its left end (top centre) is a carriage repair shop, carriage sidings, two coal sidings and a canal wharf siding, which was open to public goods traffic.

SOUTH OF SALTLEY

10.   This is Proof House Junction and it is immediately south of Curzon Street Goods Depot. It is near the right border of map II. Our route runs to the right of the flyover, which was completed in 1896 to take LNWR Aston trains over their Rugby-London route. The two Curzon Street boxes (No. 1 is seen in 1949) were replaced in 1966, by one which worked until 1989. (R.S.Carpenter coll.)

11.   Landor Street Junction is shown on the right of map IV and here we look south along the ex-MR line, under the route to Rugby. On the right is evidence of the MR connection to Curzon Street Depot and it is seen in August 1949. (R.S.Carpenter)

12.   A northward view features Landor Street Junction Box with the New Street lines on the left. The box opened on 15th November 1896 and closed on 24th August 1969. The DMU is on the points of the Camp Hill line. In the background is Lawley Street Box, which closed on 25th November 1973. (B.Wright)

13.   Lawley Street B Box is seen on 30th September 1967, looking towards Birmingham. It came into use on 28th May 1893 and lasted until 16th August 1970. The new goods shed opened in 1945. Lawley Street Goods Shed is in the background. (R.S.Carpenter)

14.	Lawley Goods Shed is seen on 4th June 1942, not long before its demolition. Centre is a horse-drawn cart. The building was erected in 1891, close to the site of the terminus, and was electrically lit from the start. The terminal lasted as offices until the bombing of November 1940. (SLS coll.)

15.	Lawley Street Freightliner Terminal opened on 20th January 1969 and by March 1970 170 containers were handled daily. No. 57001 is seen at work on 31st October 2003. The original facilities had closed on 6th February 1987. (P.D.Shannon)

Saltley Engine Sheds

16.   There were three sheds joined together and they are on map V, south of Duddleston Mill Road. The south facade is evident on 2nd March 1935, with unusually unhelpful staff instructions. (H.C.Casserley)

17.   The LMS acquired three Beyer-Garratt 2-6-6-2Ts in 1927 and a further 30 in 1930, after successful trials on coal trains. No. 47994 was recorded taking coal on 29th April 1956. (H.C.Casserley)

18.   The results of Nazi bombing are evident on 13th August 1940, when class 2F 0-6-0 No. 2994 was pictured. It was a MR product in 1876. The allocation here was 180 engines in 1950. (Milepost 92½)

19.   This northward view is during the transition from steam to diesel power. The code was 21A in 1948-63 and 2E until closure to steam in 1967. On the left are the coaling tower and the ash plant. The water tank is on the extreme right. The three sheds had turntables making them all roundhouses. (Colour-Rail.com)

Saltley Junction

20.	Three large gas works and a generating station were operated by Birmingham Corporation until nationalisation in 1948-49. Gas holders appear on map V and in the background of some photographs. Here class 5 4-6-0 no. 44841 runs through smoke from Saltley Gas Works on 5th September 1962. (B.W.L.Brooksbank)

21.	The gas works were massive and consumed about 600,000 tons of coal per annum by 1949, most of it coming by rail by that time. They were in use until 1969, when larger oil-reforming works were built elsewhere. The photograph was taken on 25th April 1954 and includes Duddeston Road Signal Box, which was in use from 23rd September 1888 until 1st October 1955. (D.J.Norton)

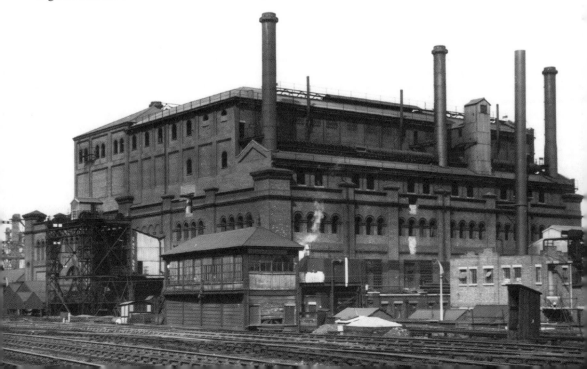

Saltley Locomotive Maintenance Depot

22.　　It is seen from Saltley Power Signal Box in 2002, with nos 66143 and 66064 in attendance. This eastward view has Landor Street Junction just beyond the right border. Duddeston Junction was the connection to the Depot, which closed officially on 22nd April 2005. (A.J.Castledine)

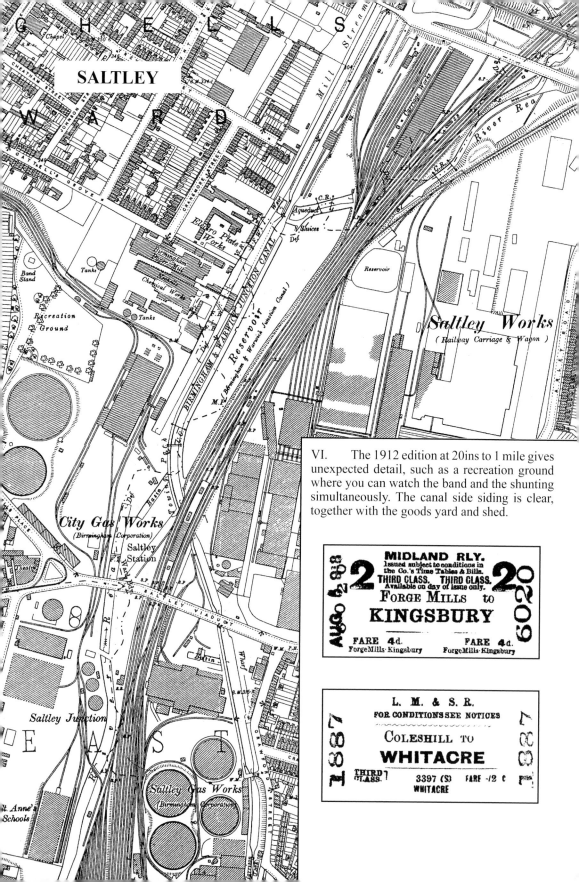

SALTLEY

Saltley Works
(Railway Carriage & Wagon)

City Gas Works
(Birmingham Corporation)

Saltley
R. Station

Saltley Junction

Saltley Gas Works
(Birmingham Corporation)

VI.　　The 1912 edition at 20ins to 1 mile gives unexpected detail, such as a recreation ground where you can watch the band and the shunting simultaneously. The canal side siding is clear, together with the goods yard and shed.

AUG 12 88

MIDLAND RLY.
Issued subject to conditions in
the Co.'s Time Tables & Bills.
2 THIRD CLASS.　THIRD CLASS. **20**
Available on day of issue only.
6020

FORGE MILLS to
KINGSBURY

FARE **4**d.　　　FARE **4**d.
ForgeMills-Kingsbury　　　ForgeMills-Kingsbury

1887

L. M. & S. R.
FOR CONDITIONS SEE NOTICES

COLESHILL TO
WHITACRE

THIRD
CLASS.　　3397 (S)　FARE -/2 C
WHITACRE

23.   We have three photographs taken on 25th October 1964. The station was for passengers only and was open from 1st October 1854 until 4th March 1968. (R.S.Carpenter)

24.   This is the view north, towards Water Orton, at the foot of the steps down from Saltley Viaduct. The box and the new station opened in 1899; the former closed on 24th August 1969. (R.S.Carpenter)

25.   Looking south, we note that the toilets were remote from the entrance, in the interest of modesty. The track and the platform both show evidence of a bridge underneath. It was over the Birmingham & Warwick Junction Canal. (R.S.Carpenter)

26.   Another northward view and this includes class 2P 2-6-0 no. 46448 and Saltley Sidings Signal Box, on 25th July 1964. (P.Shoesmith/J.Whitehouse coll.)

NORTH OF SALTLEY
Nechells Power Station

27.   The first generator was a temporary one of 22mW in World War I. One of 75mW was created in 1922-25. On the exchange siding approach on 7th September 1971 is RSH 0-6-0T no. 7684. (A.C.Hartless)

28.   The same locomotive is seen on 12th July 1970 outside the 200mW Nechells B Station, which was completed in 1954. After leaving here, we pass under the Aston to Stetchford line and south of the bridge was built Washwood Heath Sidings No. 1 Box. (A.C.Hartless)

Washwood Heath

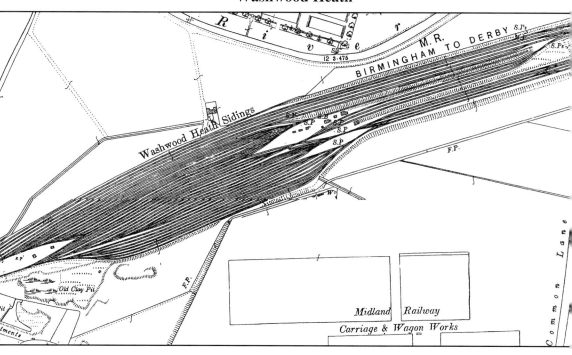

VII.   The 1904 edition at 15ins to 1 mile reveals the extent of the marshalling yards by that time.

29.   The Corporation's third gas works was called Nechells and could consume 1500 tons of coal daily in winter. Also here was the fourth gas works and it was also called Nechells. It was a high pressure naptha reforming plant supplied by tanker trains and completed in the mid-1960s. The holders were among the biggest in Europe and were completed 40 years earlier for coal gas. The view includes Washwood Heath Sidings No. 1 Box, which opened in 1899 and was a shunting frame from 24th August 1969. No. 47100 is working the 10.30 Birmingham New Street to Norwich on 15th August 1986. (J.Whitehouse)

30.　　No. 42855 is northbound with a parcels train on 5th September 1962 and passes Washwood Heath Up Yard. The Corporation once had over 2000 wagons to transport coal to its gasworks and generators. The up sidings increased to number 27 and they had access at both ends. (B.W.L.Brooksbank)

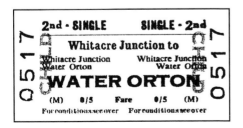

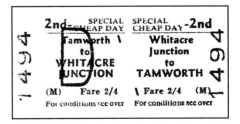

31.   In the early 1980s locomotive haulage returned to some Midlands-East Anglia services. No. 31442 passes Washwood Heath yard with the 10.30 Birmingham New Street to Norwich train on 16th February 1987. (P.Shannon)

32.   Washwood Heath yard lost most of its marshalling activity to Bescot in the 1970s, but later became a node for the national Speedlink Coal network. No. 37149 departs to the east with loaded coal hoppers on the same day. The A47 dominates this scene and the next one. (P.Shannon)

33. Passing the sidings for Bromford Bridge steelworks on the approach to Washwood Heath yard are nos 20154 and 20005 with the 07.30 March-Cardiff scrap metal train on 3rd July 1987. The track that this train was using was bidirectionally signalled to allow trains from the east to enter Washwood Heath yard without crossing over the main running lines. (P.Shannon)

BROMFORD BRIDGE RACECOURSE

34. There was a station here called "Bromford Forge" from May 1842 to May 1843. A new one on the site opened as named above on 9th March 1896, but for race traffic only. This poor view shows the rural environment, as ex-MR class 3 0-6-0 plods west on 18th August 1928. (R.S.Carpenter coll.)

35. A different angle on the same day includes sidings where traffic was sorted for nearby private sidings. The fence near the name board was of a style widely used by the MR. (R.S.Carpenter coll.)

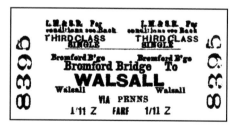

36.   The station is seen on 5th September 1962; it was not used after 28th June 1965. Quadruple track ran from Saltley almost to Water Orton. Two up trains are signalled. The box was in use from 1917 to 1969. (B.W.L.Brooksbank)

37.   A panorama from 3rd August 1969 features power line upgrades and commercial rail traffic. Private sidings served by the end of the century included Esso Petroleum, Dunlop and Corus Engineering Steels. Much further east was the Jaguar car terminal. (B.Wright)

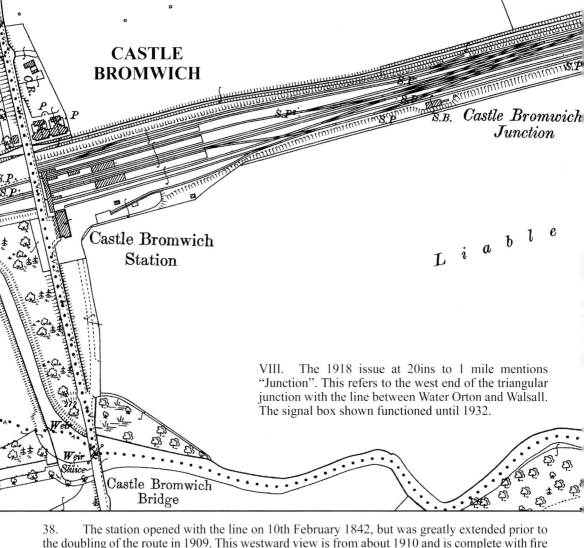

CASTLE BROMWICH

S.B. Castle Bromwich Junction

Castle Bromwich
Station

Liable

Castle Bromwich
Bridge

Weir

Weir Sluice

VIII. The 1918 issue at 20ins to 1 mile mentions "Junction". This refers to the west end of the triangular junction with the line between Water Orton and Walsall. The signal box shown functioned until 1932.

38.   The station opened with the line on 10th February 1842, but was greatly extended prior to the doubling of the route in 1909. This westward view is from about 1910 and is complete with fire buckets on the gents. (R.S.Carpenter coll.)

39.   Class 2P 4-4-0 no. 517 speeds west on 5th May 1936, probably working from Derby to Birmingham. The east ends of the two goods yard sidings are evident. There was no crane; the one seen was mobile. (H.C.Casserley)

40.   The exterior was decorated for the British Industries Fair on 28th April 1951 and the shadows added to the polychromatic brickwork appearance. (R.S.Carpenter)

41.   The up platforms were recorded on the same day, along with multi-lingual signage, together with one for a buffet, an imported foreign word which did not need changing. (R.S.Carpenter)

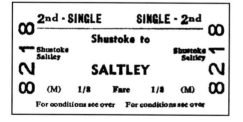

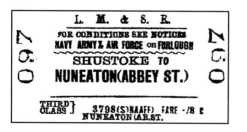

42.   Running on the up goods line a few weeks later is a "Black Five" 4-6-0 with a Bristol to Sheffield express. Few will see the choice of tongues on offer. (R.S.Carpenter)

43.   The same fair was on the headboard in April 1957, when visitors could be impressed by a diesel-electric hauling their train. It is diesel electric no. 10203. (Colour-Rail.com)

WEST OF WATER ORTON

IX.   The 1918 issue is at 15ins to 1 mile. Until the 1950s, the yard was so busy that it needed four shunting engines on duty 24 hours per day. The diverging lines on the left formed part of the triangle, with the Walsall route at the top. The River Tame and the ancient bridge over it are top right.

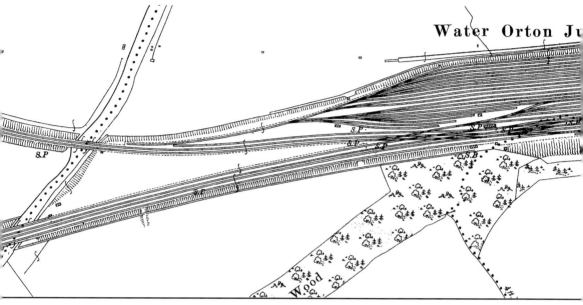

44.   Cruising on the up goods on 6th August 1952, an 0-6-0 approaches the station and gives us a glance at the yards. They ceased to be used after 1968 and the number of tracks on the south side of the triangle was later reduced from four to three. The other sides were singled. (D.J.Norton)

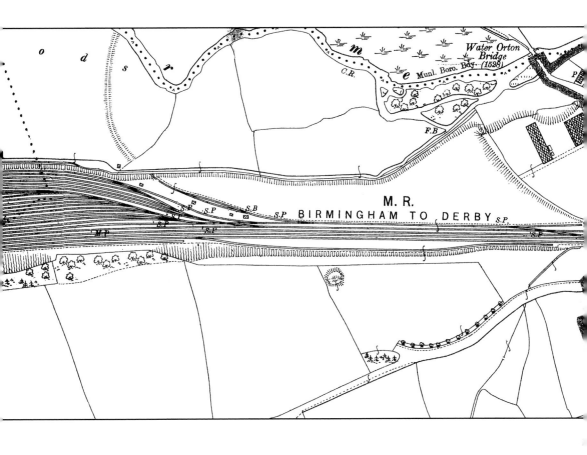

M. R.
BIRMINGHAM TO DERBY

Water Orton Bridge (152)
Munl. Boro. Bdy.

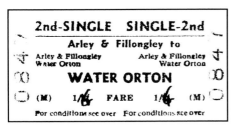

2nd-SINGLE   SINGLE-2nd
Arley & Fillongley to
Arley & Fillongley   Arley & Fillongley
Water Orton   Water Orton
WATER ORTON
(M)   1/4   FARE   1/4   (M)
For conditions see over   For conditions see over

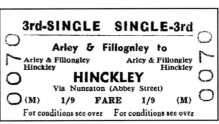

3rd-SINGLE   SINGLE-3rd
Arley & Fillongley to
Arley & Fillongley   Arley & Fillongley
Hinckley   Hinckley
HINCKLEY
Via Nuneaton (Abbey Street)
(M)   1/9   FARE   1/9   (M)
For conditions see over   For conditions see over

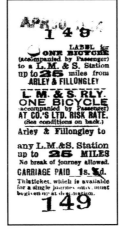

APR 1 49
1 4 9
LABEL for
ONE BICYCLE
(accompanied by Passenger)
to a L.M. & S. Station
up to **25** miles from
ARLEY & FILLONGLEY
L.M. & S. RLY.
ONE BICYCLE
(accompanied by Passenger)
AT CO.'S LTD. RISK RATE.
(See conditions on back.)
Arley & Fillongley to
any L.M.&S. Station
up to **25** MILES
No break of journey allowed.
CARRIAGE PAID 1s. 5d.
This ticket, which is available
for a single journey only, must
be given up at destination.
149

WATER ORTON

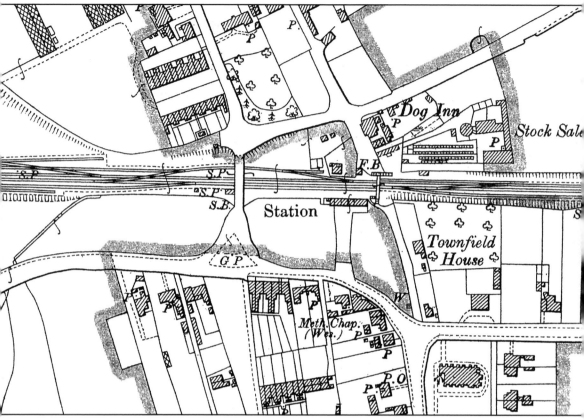

X.   This overlaps the previous map, but is scaled at 25ins to 1 mile, to show details of the original station, and is from 1903.

45.   The new station had a single island platform, which came into use on 3rd May 1909. This is a view east along it in about 1930. On the right is the goods yard, which opened on 17th May 1908 and closed on 7th March 1966. (Stations UK)

46. Two class 8F 2-8-0s were photographed from the south end of the footbridge on 3rd May 1966. No. 48063 is hauling freight towards the north, while no. 48674 is running in from the east. (Colour-Rail.com)

XI. The 1924 edition includes the enlarged goods yard and the quadrupling. It is scaled at 15ins to 1 mile.

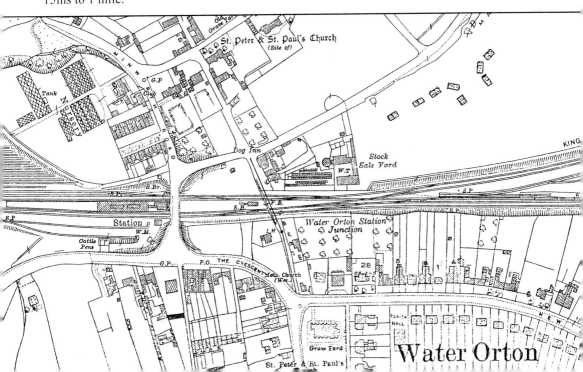

47.	This eastward panorama is from 26th April 1975 and includes no. 47288 and also the divergence of the Tamworth and Nuneaton lines. The box came into use on 12th May 1963, its MR predecessor being to the left of the camera. It was called Water Orton East and closed on 10th August 1969. (Colour-Rail.com)

48.	The bridge in the last photograph was the viewpoint for this photograph of no. 31176 on 5th June 1980. Replacement track was under construction on the Tamworth route on the left, following installation of a new drainage system. (A.C.Hartless)

49. Sadly, the eastern elevation was partially obscured when "Peak" class no. 45049 *The Staffordshire Regiment* was recorded northbound with a Freightliner on 1st March 1984. (B.Morrison)

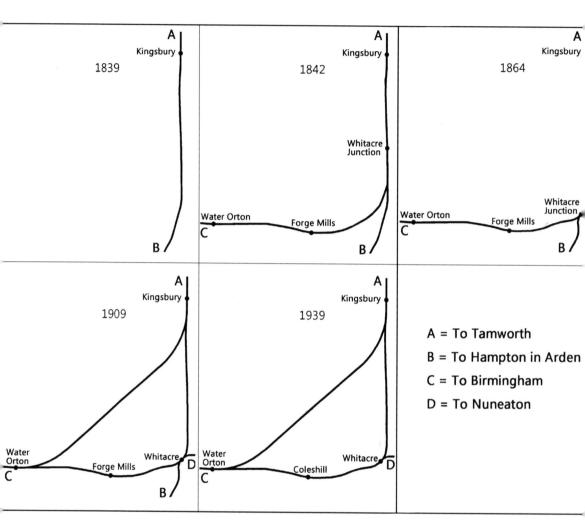

XII. The evolution of the railways of the area is shown with diagrams which indicate the years of major change. (N.Langridge)

Other views of Water Orton can be found in pictures 29 to 33 in the Middleton Press album *North of Birmingham* which includes the routes to Bescot and Lichfield.

KINGSBURY

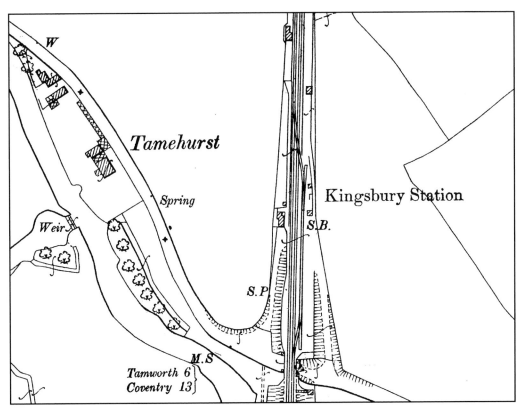

XIII.   We run north from hereon and see our next stop on the 1903 edition. There was road access on both sides of the line, but the platforms were staggered. The signal box (S.B.) shown was in use in 1898-1908. Its replacement lasted until 10th August 1969.

50.   Looking south in 1956, we see the main building plus a parcels shed created from a retired van. The population was 2747 in 1901 and 6358 in 1961. Left is the goods yard, which closed on 6th July 1964. (R.S.Carpenter)

51.　　Passing with a coal train on 16th April 1959 is class 4F 0-6-0 no. 43940. The ornate finials and elaborate chimney are noteworthy. (R.S.Carpenter)

52.　　A northward panorama in the same era shows that the station master could survey his territory easily. Passenger service was withdrawn on 4th March 1968. (R.S.Carpenter)

53.　　　Details in another 1950s photograph include an LMS "Hawkseye" style nameboard and oil lamps. The tiny porch is unusual and is shown as out of use in the previous view. (R.M.Casserley)

NORTH OF KINGSBURY

54.   "Royal Scot" class 4-6-0 no. 46141 *The North Staffordshire Regiment* leaves Kingsbury Colliery branch sidings in about 1962, with a southbound coal train. The yard has six parallel sidings for marshalling purposes. (R.S.Carpenter)

XIV.   A 1ins to 1 mile map extract from 1946 has Kingsbury on the left with the mineral line curving to the right to a colliery, which is Birch Coppice. Baddesley Colliery was near the right border.

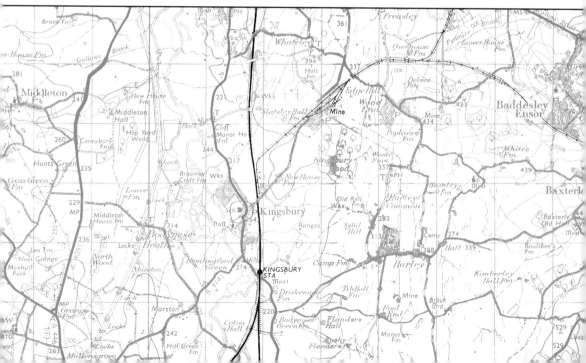

55.   Two Colas class 47s run by with a Boston to Washwood Heath steel train on 9th July 2009. The Kingsbury branch served the European Metal Recycling premises, hence the scrap train. At the end of the three-mile long branch was the TNT VW Group Logistics. (J.Whitehouse)

56.   No. 66144 arrives at Kingsbury sidings with the 11.33 Humber (Immingham) to Kingsbury oil train on 13th June 2011. It will set back into the sidings on the right in order to gain access to the petroleum distribution terminal. Once it has completed the manoeuvre, the container train on the Birch Coppice branch in the distance will be able to pull out on to the main line. It has come from the Warwickshire Oil Storage Co. (P.D.Shannon)

57.   Birch Coppice Colliery started as Hall End Colliery in 1878 and was developed with several shafts being sunk. Some were deepened, but closure came in 1988. *Birch Coppice* was photographed in 1929. (SLS coll.)

58.   We are near the end of the branch and this is the Volkswagen parts depot. A long rake of Cargowaggons is being shunted by a road-rail vehicle on 22nd August 2006. (P.D.Shannon)

59.　　Baddesley Colliery had two railway connections. The 1937 Beyer-Peacock 0-4-0+0-4-0T is crossing the A5 on their line north to a canal wharf and connection to the West Coast Main Line, northwest of Atherstone. Named *William Francis*, the locomotive retired to Bressingham Museum in 1968. (P.Shoesmith/J.Whitehouse coll.)

60.　　Nearest is Hunslet 0-6-0ST *No. 1*, works no. 2859 from 1943. In the background is their Beyer-Peacock. The pit closed in 1989. (P.Shoesmith/J.Whitehouse coll.)

WILNECOTE

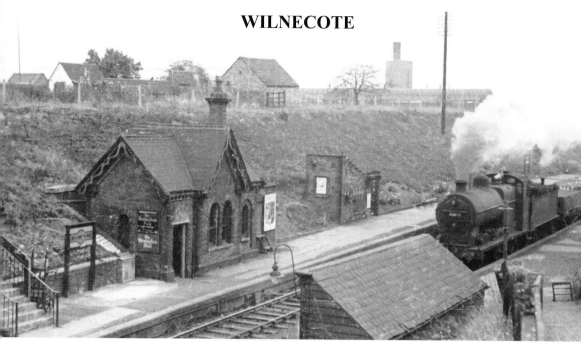

61.   A southward panorama in 1949 includes a class 4F 0-6-0. The station opened on 16th March 1842 and had the suffix "& Fazeley" until 1st April 1904. (Stations UK)

62.   The proximity of the station to the widened road is emphasised in this March 1967 view. The steps up to the road are on the right. (R.S.Carpenter)

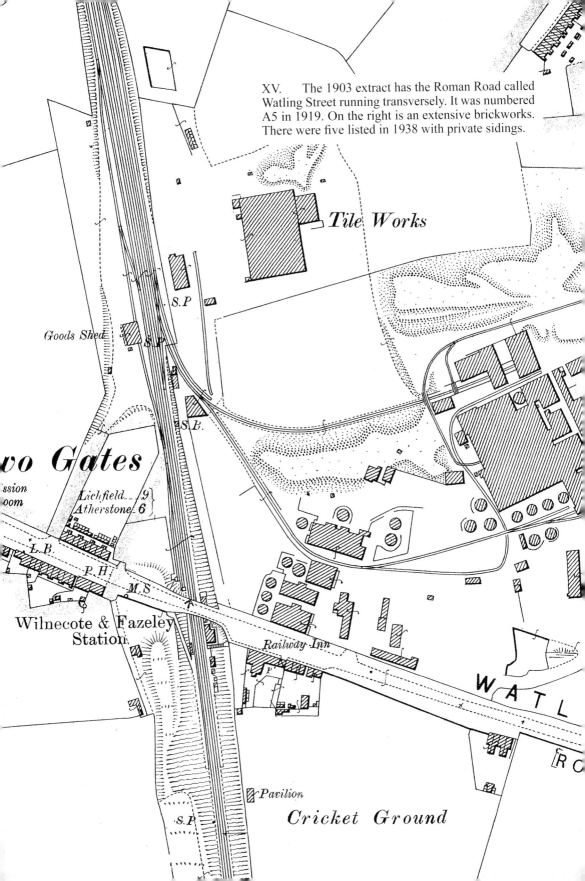

XV. The 1903 extract has the Roman Road called Watling Street running transversely. It was numbered A5 in 1919. On the right is an extensive brickworks. There were five listed in 1938 with private sidings.

Tile Works

S.P.

Goods Shed

S.P.

S.B.

vo Gates

ssion
oom

Lichfield 9
Atherstone 6

L.B.

P.H.

M.S.

Wilnecote & Fazeley
Station

Railway Inn

W A T L

R○

Pavilion

S.P.

Cricket Ground

63.   The up platform did not have steps, but an inclined path. This is evident on the left of this 1970 view. (Stations UK)

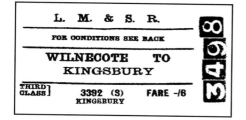

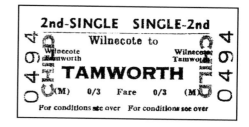

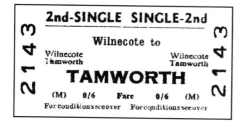

64. The ticket office was adjacent to Atherstone Street, which was downgraded from A5 to A5404. The station maintained a substantial commuter traffic to Birmingham. (R.S.Carpenter)

65. The buildings were lost, but platforms were maintained for four coaches each side. No. 170522 will have just run over the River Anker on Tamworth Viaduct on 21st December 2013, while running from Nottingham to Cardiff. (J.Whitehouse)

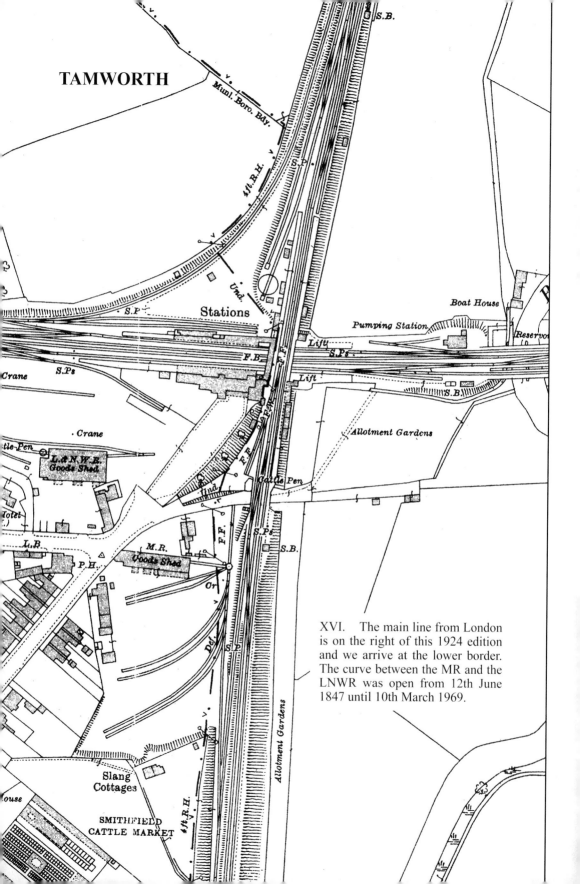

TAMWORTH

XVI.   The main line from London is on the right of this 1924 edition and we arrive at the lower border. The curve between the MR and the LNWR was open from 12th June 1847 until 10th March 1969.

66. The MR part of the station is behind the cart, while the LNWR section is behind the carriages. The main line section was termed Low Level in 1924-71. (P.Laming coll.)

67. This northward panorama from 1950 includes part of the signal box, which was in use from 8th August 1925 until 10th August 1969. The short siding on the left served the cattle dock. (Stations UK)

68.   Running north in 1952 is class 3F 0-6-0 no. 43294. The cattle pen is in the right background, but its siding had gone. There was no usable platform under the gas lamp. (P.Kingston/R.S.Carpenter coll.)

69.   Class 8F 2-8-0 no. 48176 is southbound with freight. The pitched roofs each side of the locomotive are over the hydraulic lift shafts, used for luggage and parcels to and from Low Level. The dock line had gone and the platform was lengthened over its site in 1962. (Milepost 92½)

For other views of this station, please see the Middleton Press album *Rugby to Stafford.*

70.   Goods traffic ceased here on 8th September 1969, but in the meantime major rebuilding took place. This is the scene on 20th December 1961, as class 3F 0-6-0 no. 43709 works hard with a down coal train. The opening of the new premises took place on 24th September 1962. Around 2000 mail bags changed trains here each night at that time. About 20 postmen were needed. (B.W.L.Brooksbank)

71.   The results of a further rebuild were recorded on 2nd July 2013, as no. 37405 ran north with an inspection saloon. All the platforms were then fit for 12 coaches and electric lifts were in use. Some platforms were earlier fit for 15. (J.Whitehouse)

FORGE MILLS

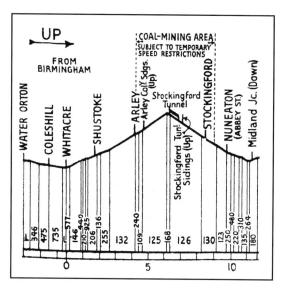

We return south to join the Nuneaton route 1½ mile east of Water Orton. An interesting note is to be found above the summit.

XVII. The 1903 edition shows the name used until 29th July 1923, when it was changed to Coleshill. The first station with this name was on the line south to Hampton. (See picture 111).

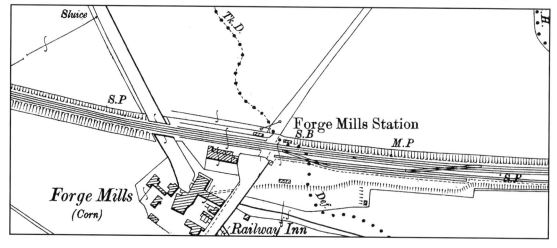

72.　　　The name carried the suffix "For Coleshill" from 1st November 1849 until 1st April 1904 and so we assume that this view is after that period, but before 1923. When the station opened in 1842, it was on the only route between Birmingham and Tamworth. (P.Laming coll.)

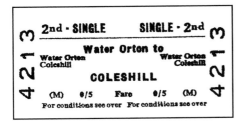

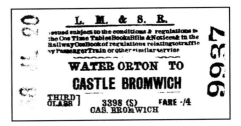

COLESHILL

73.   A DMU departs for Birmingham New Street, sometime in the 1960s. Two sidings had been provided by 1938 for power stations. The first one was built in the late 1920s. Public freight traffic ceased on 6th July 1964. The plant in the background is a Gas Lurgi, not a power station. It was run by Coleshill Distillers (Carbon Dioxide) Ltd in the 1970s. (M.Whitehouse)

74.   The down side waiting room and parcel store were to a design used elsewhere by the MR. The frontage was similar to a domestic weather forecasting device used prior to the coming of radio. Passenger service ceased on 4th March 1968. (R.S.Carpenter)

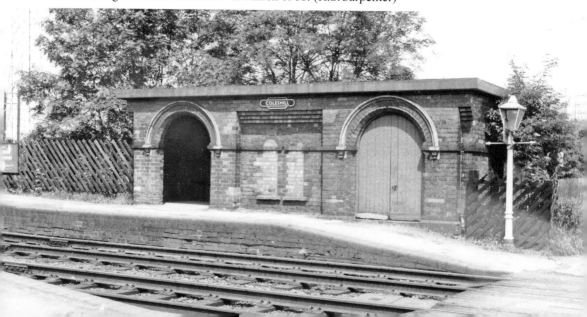

75.   A photograph from August 1969 features the box, which was in use from 3rd December 1939 until 10th August 1969. The historic signal post was about to be removed. (B.Wright)

COLESHILL PARKWAY

76.   After almost 40 years, this new station was built on the site of the original one and was opened on 19th August 2007. The stairs wind round the lift shaft and wind is unwelcome on wet days if users of the former are to remain dry. (A.C.Hartless)

77.   Both pictures are from 29th July 2008 and here we see no. 170637 working the 15.51 Birmingham New Street to Leicester. The level crossing had been replaced by an over bridge. The lower signs advise passengers (sorry - customers) to change here for Birmingham International Airport and the National Exhibition Centre. (A.C.Hartless)

EAST OF COLESHILL

78.   Two power stations were built at Hams Hall in the 1940s-50s, but were demolished by 1993. Class 8F 2-8-0 no. 48687 with coal empties from the power station is approaching the Water Orton to Whitacre slow line via Coleshill and nears Whitacre Junction in the early 1960s. (R.S.Carpenter)

79.   Hams Hall intermodel terminal opened in 1997. Its main purpose was to handle Channel Tunnel traffic but the Channel Tunnel business failed to grow and instead Hams Hall became another West Midlands railhead for deep-sea containers from ports such as Felixstowe and Southampton. No. 66710 shunts intermodal traffic from Felixstowe at Hams Hall on 23rd October 2002. (P.D.Shannon)

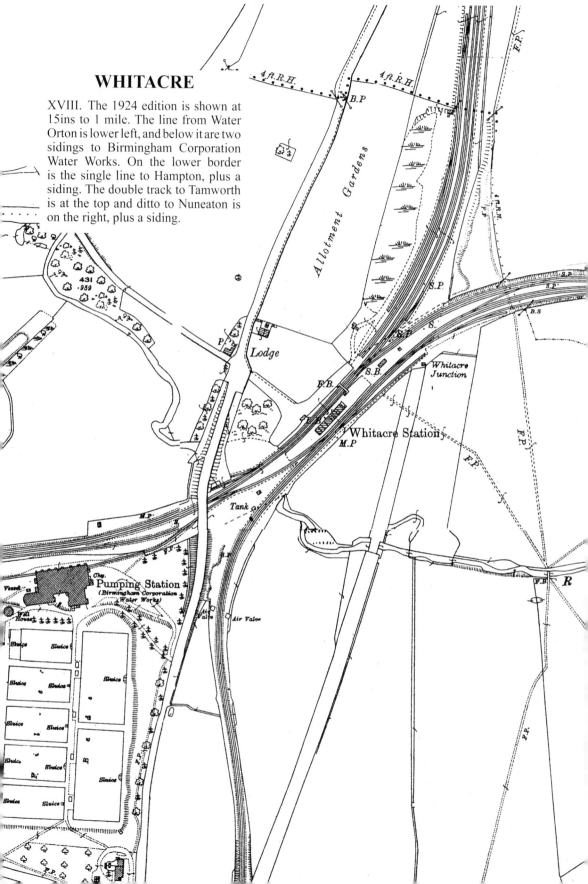

WHITACRE

XVIII. The 1924 edition is shown at 15ins to 1 mile. The line from Water Orton is lower left, and below it are two sidings to Birmingham Corporation Water Works. On the lower border is the single line to Hampton, plus a siding. The double track to Tamworth is at the top and ditto to Nuneaton is on the right, plus a siding.

80.   We look southwest from the footbridge in 1949 and see the water works in the distance. The main buildings are on the island platform. The word "junction" was used prior to 1st October 1904. (R.S.Carpenter)

81.   The station came into use on 1st November 1864 the first one being further north, as shown on the diagram XII, prior to picture 50. The photograph is from 1967.(Stations UK)

82.   The bridge in the previous view is the view point for this panorama from 3rd August 1969. Our journey to Nuneaton continues on the route on the right. The signal box was in use from 17th December 1939 until 10th August 1969. (B.Wright)

83.   A broader view on the same day shows one less signal arm than in 1967. This is because the goods line had been removed. The goods yard closed on 1st March 1965 and passenger service ceased on 4th March 1968. North Box had functioned from 1897 to 1958 and was beyond the border of the map. (B.Wright)

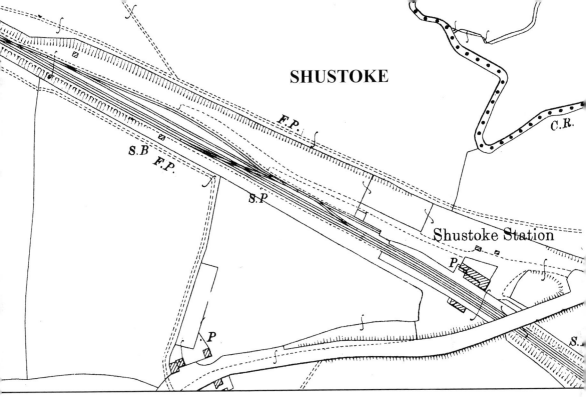

SHUSTOKE

XIX.   Another 1903 map and this reveals the great length of the goods yard. The population increased from 420 in 1901 to 547 in 1961.

84.   The size of the yard is confirmed from the road bridge and the signal box is in the distance. This was in use from 16th April 1899 until 10th August 1969. Goods service ceased on 24th July 1961. (P.Laming coll.)

85.　　Typical MR fencing was still present in 1956, as were LMS signs. Other items from the past are a ladder to aid lamp lighting and a Royal Mail letter box in the wall. (Stations UK)

British Rlys(M)For
conditions see back
Third Class Single

Coleshill

Coleshill To
SHUSTOKE
Shustoke

-18 Z

1646

British Rlys(M)For
conditions see back
Third Class Single

Coleshill

Coleshill
Shustoke

-18 Z

1646

1010 MAR 10.
8947
M.R. Available for RETURN
on the day of issue or following
day or from a Saturday to the
following Monday night

Birmingham to
FORGE MILLS
THIRD Class
(SEE BACK)

86.   Class 4P 2-6-4T no. 42186 calls with a Leicester to Birmingham semi-fast service, but no date is recorded. Five differing 4P designs were produced, between 1927 and 1945. (R.S.Carpenter)

87.   This sad view of weeds in the rain in March 1968 preludes the demise of the station. This took place on the 4th of that month. (W.A.Camwell/SLS coll.)

EAST OF SHUSTOKE

88.   Daw Mill Colliery had its first shaft sunk in 1956-59 and its second in 1969-71. Production began in April 1965. By 2008, it had 608 employees, but it closed on 7th March 2013, following a fire. This 1974 eastward view had the four parallel sidings on the left and behind the camera were the reception and departure sidings. All were on the north side of the main line. (P.Crome)

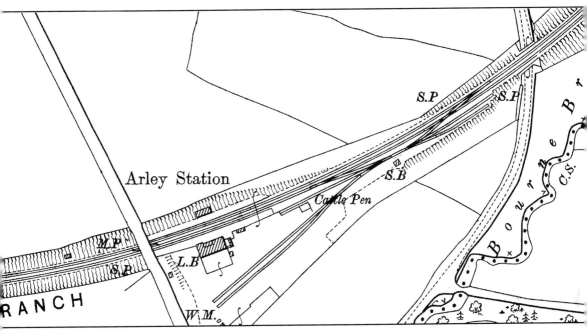

XX.   The line reaches almost 400ft above sea level here. Unusual on this 1903 edition are two short headshunts. The valley side would not allow one long one, but one had gone by 1930.

89.   An eastward view pre-World War I includes the signal box which was open from 1898 to 6th October 1968. There were 201 residents in 1901. (P.Laming coll.)

90. The station closed to passengers on 7th November 1960 and was photographed in 1961 as "Jubilee" class 4-6-0 no. 45619 ran through with freight. The goods yard closed on 4th January 1965. The route was closed for almost all of 1949 and again for six months in 2013. (Stations UK)

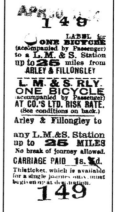

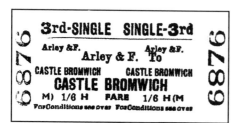

91.　　The building became a private house and is seen on 1st July 1983 as the 15.43 from Leicester speeds by. The bridge carried the B4098, formerly the A51. (A.C.Hartless)

XXI.　　Arley Colliery layout is shown in 1924 at 15ins to 1 mile. A platform for use by miners was provided on the main line between about 1917 and 1945, but it is not shown. The sidings were in use from 1876 to 1964.

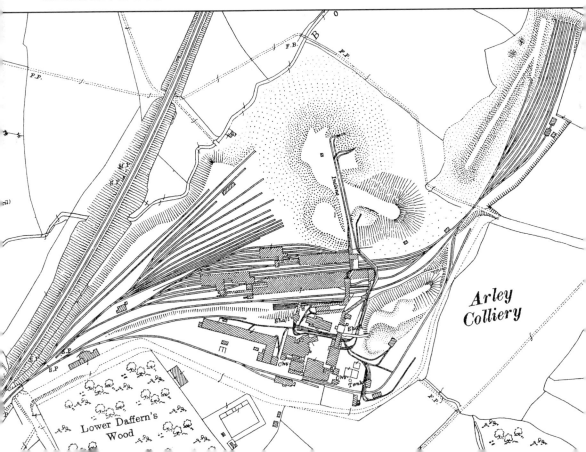

Arley
Colliery

Lower Daffern's
Wood

WEST OF STOCKINGFORD

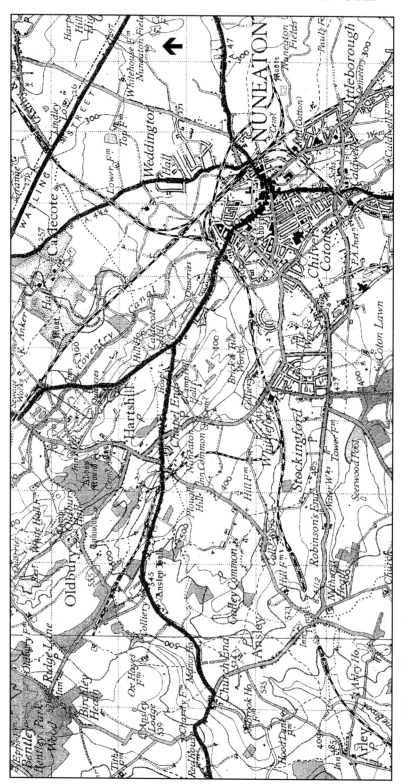

XXII. The 709yd long Arley Tunnel is on the left of this 1946 map at 1ins to 1 mile. Ansley Hall and Colliery are both south of Oldbury (upper left), near the end of the branch. Coal was won from 1876 to 1959 and a public goods yard functioned for most of that time at the end of the branch, known as Green's Wharf.

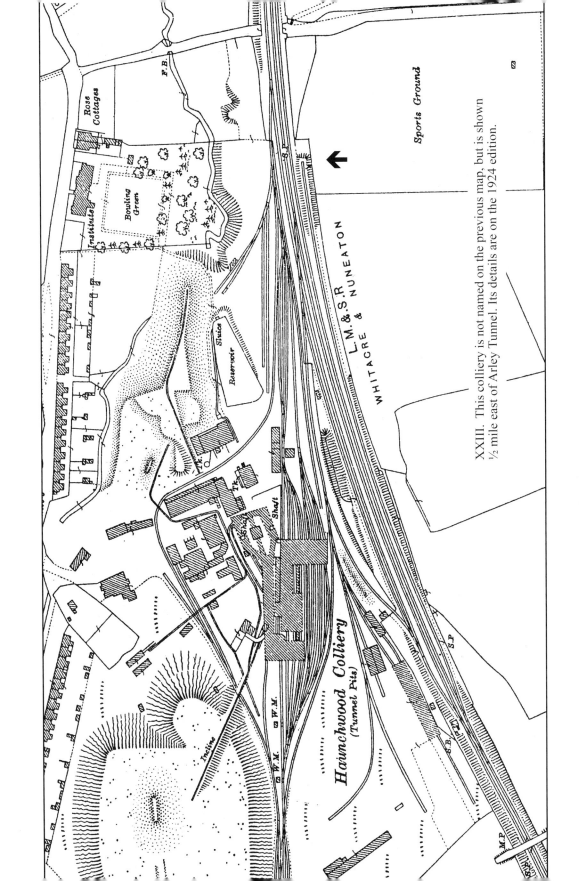

Rose Cottages

F.B.

Institute

Bowling Green

Reservoir

Sluice

Incline

W.M.

W.M.

W.M.

Shaft

T.

Hawnwood Colliery
(Tunnel Pits)

S.P.

S.B.

M.P.

S.P.

L.M.&S.R.
WHITACRE & NUNEATON

Sports Ground

XXIII. This colliery is not named on the previous map, but is shown ½ mile east of Arley Tunnel. Its details are on the 1924 edition.

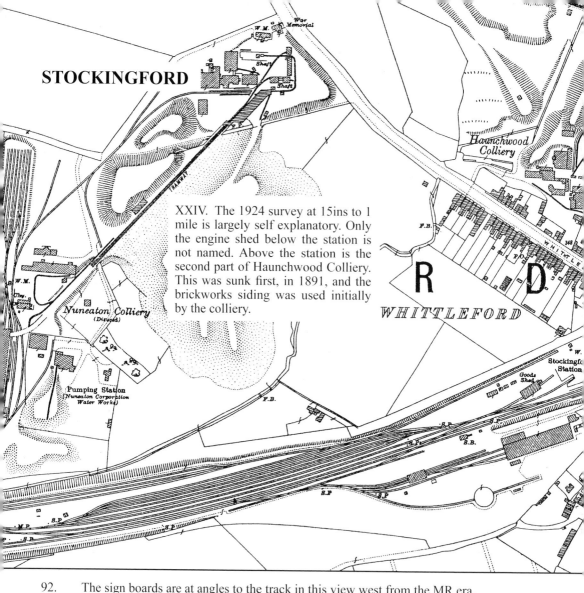

STOCKINGFORD

XXIV. The 1924 survey at 15ins to 1 mile is largely self explanatory. Only the engine shed below the station is not named. Above the station is the second part of Haunchwood Colliery. This was sunk first, in 1891, and the brickworks siding was used initially by the colliery.

92.   The sign boards are at angles to the track in this view west from the MR era. (P.Laming coll.)

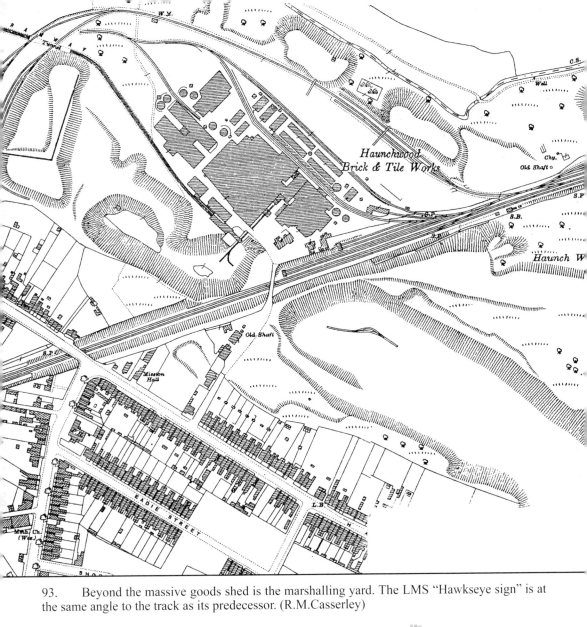

93.   Beyond the massive goods shed is the marshalling yard. The LMS "Hawkseye sign" is at the same angle to the track as its predecessor. (R.M.Casserley)

94.　　In the background is the goods yard, which was in use until 11th April 1960. It had a 30cwt crane in its shed. This 1961 picture includes signals which were worked from Stockingford Branch Junction Box, which was open from 7th March 1897 to 10th August 1969. Station Box served from 1875 until 1934. (Stations UK)

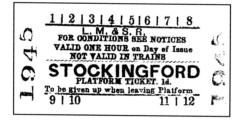

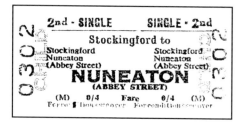

95.   The locomotive shed closed on 7th November 1932 but continued in use as a signing on point until 1960. We are looking towards the southwest corner of the shed with the main line running from Birmingham to Nuneaton behind it. In the background are the chimneys of Haunchwood brick and tile works. In the foreground lies the remains of the turntable. The depot did not show on the 1903 survey, as it opened that year. The photograph is from 7th October 1962. (R.S.Carpenter)

96.   Class 5 4-6-0 no. 45040 passes through with a parcels train on 9th August 1963, with the brickworks in the background. Passenger service ceased here on 4th March 1968 and no trace now remains of the station. (Colour-Rail.com)

NUNEATON ABBEY STREET

XXV. Lower left on the page is the start of a mineral line, the extent of which is shown on map XXII. The 1914 edition has our route at the bottom. The Ashby route at the top left was in use from 1873 to 1971.

To enjoy more views please see
HST Cab Ride
Birmingham New Street to Derby
available from Middleton Prerss.

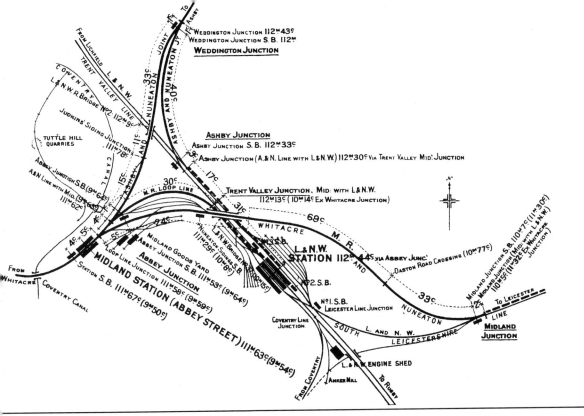

XXVI. The MR 1916 diagram reveals the complex route for stopping trains and the easy one for expresses and freight trains. The Ashby line (top) lost its passenger service in 1931. The spur between the MR and the LNWR opened in 1880, but was not used regularly. The bridge over the main line closed in February 1992, having been used mainly for freight.

97. A view towards Leicester on 24th May 1952 reveals a total lack of weather protection. Even the steps to Midland Road are exposed.
(R.S.Carpenter)

98. This station replaced the original one on 1st September 1873, which was seven chains to the west. The new one acquired the suffix ABBEY STREET on 2nd June 1924 and is seen on 14th April 1957.
(H.C.Casserley)

99. A panorama from the top of the west steps shows short platforms. The cattle pens are evident, as is the loading gauge over the short siding.
(Stations UK)

100. We are about to pass under Midland Road and approach the junction. The station closed to passengers on 4th March 1968.
(Milepost 92½)

101. DMUs were introduced on the Birmingham to Leicester service in March 1958. This example was recorded from Midland Road in mist in March 1968. (W.A.Camwell/SLS coll.)

102. The junction signal box was lost by fire created by vandals on 25th March 1993. It was opened on 1st November 1925 and had closed on 21st February 1992. Class 4F 0-6-0 no. 44103 is on a coal train. The other locomotive is a class G2 0-8-0 no. 49342. (R.S.Carpenter)

103. The Nuneaton avoiding line closed in February 1992. No. 37711 comes off it at Abbey Junction with the 11.35 Leicester Braunstone Gate to Cardiff Tidal scrap metal train on 2nd November 1991. The goods yard had been on the right, but it closed on 2nd October 1972. A 10-ton crane had been available. (P.D.Shannon)

104. A new flyover at Nuneaton enabled cross-country trains to avoid conflicting with those on the West Coast main line. Unlike the previous Nuneaton avoiding line, it was routed via Nuneaton station to allow stopping passenger trains to use it. The flyover is pictured looking west on 19th April 2011. It had opened on 7th June 2004. The electrified main line can be seen below. (P.D.Shannon)

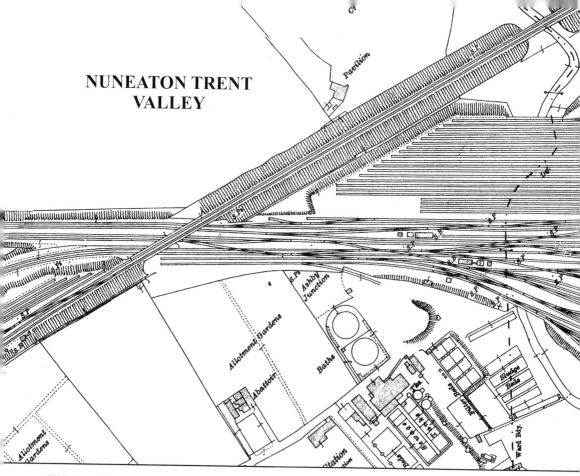

NUNEATON TRENT VALLEY

XXVII. The 1914 edition is best examined with the last diagram, as it indicates destinations of routes.

105.   A northwest view from 19th February 1960 features class G2 0-8-0 no. 49425 running near some track workers. The station was enlarged with an island platform in 1868. (D.A.Johnson)

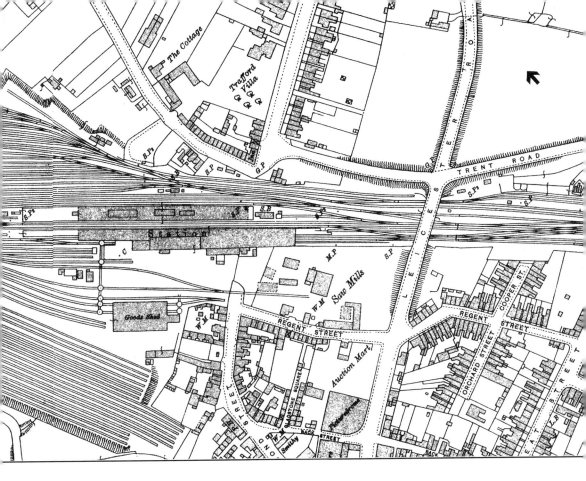

106.   The suffix TRENT VALLEY was applied from 2nd June 1924 until 5th May 1969, although the name is still used for the main line. Stranger in the camp! Buxton based Class 104 set 486 forms the 07.15hrs Birmingham to Leicester and is seen departing under a clear signal on 8th November 1983. (A.C.Hartless)

107.   No. 40013 is about to start up from the dock siding just north of platform 1. The massive ex-LNWR warehouse is beyond and is seen on 13th November 1982. (A.C.Hartless)

108.   Viewed across the sidings from platform 5, nos 25306 and 25123 are stabled at the dock siding on 8th January 1983. On the left are the holding sidings, now long gone. (A.C.Hartless)

109.   The vista is from platform 3 on 31st January 2011. Centre are nos 4 and 5 which date from 1868 and on the left are nos 6 and 7, which came into use on 7th June 2004. (Colour-Rail.com)

For other pictures of this location, please consult the *Rugby to Stafford* album.

110.   The west facade and station approach were recorded on the same day. Work was in progress to provide a new link between the east and north of England, by relaying the ex-MR route east of the station and using two bridges. This was to benefit container traffic to and from Felixstowe. (Colour-Rail.com)

MAXSTOKE GOODS
(COLESHILL)

XXVIII. The MR diagram of 1916 shows sidings not otherwise mentioned.

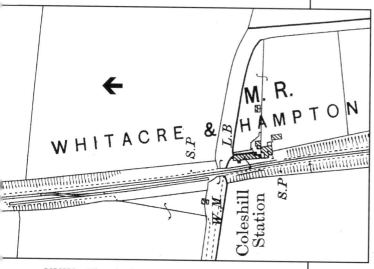

XXIX. The single siding is shown on a 1903 extract.

111. The station closed on 1st January 1917 and was complete with lamp and advertisements when photographed in 1923. Much of the track still had inside keys. (R.S.Carpenter)

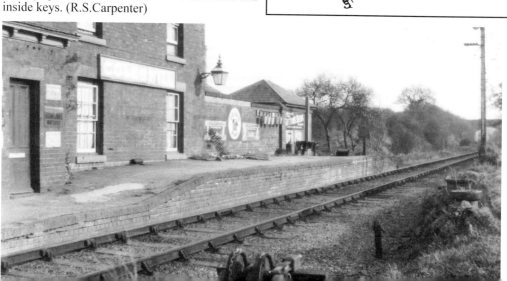

112. The lamp had gone, but the name was still on show in this later undated view. The name of the goods yard was changed to Maxstoke on 9th July 1923. A siding was opened about 2½ miles north of Hampton in around 1940 for the loading of sand for use in the construction of an airfield for the RAF. (P.Laming coll.)

113. Goods traffic was run from the north only from 24th April 1930 until closure on 30th April 1939. The relic is seen on 20th March 1954. The bridge over the River Blythe became too weak to use in January 1935. There were five other such bridges.
(P.J.Garland/
R.S.Carpenter coll.)

114. Our final view is from the same day. The route opened in 1839 and the final single track was not lifted until 1952. In the final years, both ends of the route were used for wagon storage. It then became a bird's paradise.
(R.S.Carpenter)

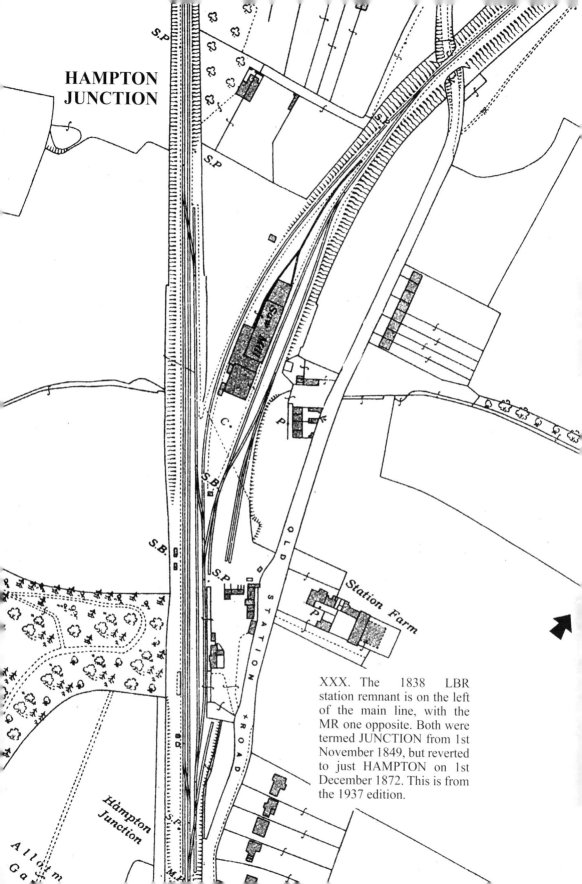

HAMPTON JUNCTION

XXX. The 1838 LBR station remnant is on the left of the main line, with the MR one opposite. Both were termed JUNCTION from 1st November 1849, but reverted to just HAMPTON on 1st December 1872. This is from the 1937 edition.

115.   The ex-MR station was recorded in March 1954, along with its cattle dock. The main line was just behind the camera. (R.S.Carpenter)

116.   The original B&DJR locomotive shed survived in use as a saw mill to be photographed in 1954. All London to Derby trains had their engines changed here, until 1842. (P.J.Garland/R.S.Carpenter coll.)

HAMPTON-IN-ARDEN

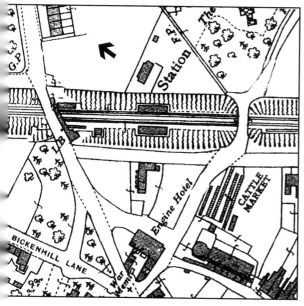

XXXI. This 1937 extract features the 1884 station. Its goods yard was beyond the right border.

117.   A link with the past was the antique ground signal, which survived to be photographed on 20th March 1954. (Milepost 92½)

118.   Looking towards Birmingham in about 1930, we find covered stairs up to a roofed footbridge. "Arden" was added in 1876, it referring to the forest in the area. (Stations UK)

119.   A view towards Coventry shows the end of the loop which runs adjacent to the goods yard, at the far end of the cutting. The locomotive is 2-6-0 no. 42979 and it is seen on 9th July 1960. (Milepost 92½)

Other views can be seen in pictures 89 to 93 in the *Rugby to Birmingham* **album.**

120.   A different angle from the opposite platform in 1959 shows the main building, which included residential accommodation for the station master. All the buildings vanished shortly before electrification in 1966 and new structures appeared. (Stations UK)

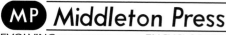

Middleton Press

EVOLVING THE ULTIMATE RAIL ENCYCLOPEDIA

Easebourne Lane, Midhurst, West Sussex.
GU29 9AZ   Tel:01730 813169
www.middletonpress.co.uk   email:info@middletonpress.co.uk
A-978 0 906520   B- 978 1 873793   C- 978 1 901706   D-978 1 904474
E- 978 1 906008   F- 978 1 908174

All titles listed below were in print at time of publication - please check current availability by looking at our website - *www.middletonpress.co.uk* or by requesting a Brochure which includes our *LATEST* RAILWAY TITLES also our TRAMWAY, TROLLEYBUS, MILITARY and COASTAL series